DATE DUE

Youth Development and Neighborhood
Influences: Challenges and Opportunities

Chalk and Phillips

Youth Development and Neighborhood Influences

Challenges and Opportunities

Summary of a Workshop

Rosemary Chalk and Deborah A. Phillips, Editors

Committee on Youth Development

Board on Children, Youth, and Families

Commission on Behavioral and Social Sciences and Education
National Research Council

Institute of Medicine

NATIONAL ACADEMY PRESS
Washington, D.C. 1996

NOTICE: The project that is the subject of this report was approved by the Governing Board of the National Research Council, whose members are drawn from the councils of the National Academy of Sciences, the National Academy of Engineering, and the Institute of Medicine. The members of the committee responsible for the report were chosen for their special competences and with regard for appropriate balance.

This report has been reviewed by a group other than the authors according to procedures approved by a Report Review Committee consisting of members of the National Academy of Sciences, the National Academy of Engineering, and the Institute of Medicine.

The National Academy of Sciences is a private, nonprofit, self-perpetuating society of distinguished scholars engaged in scientific and engineering research, dedicated to the furtherance of science and technology and to their use for the general welfare. Upon the authority of the charter granted to it by the Congress in 1863, the Academy has a mandate that requires it to advise the federal government on scientific and technical matters. Dr. Bruce M. Alberts is president of the National Academy of Sciences.

The National Academy of Engineering was established in 1964, under the charter of the National Academy of Sciences, as a parallel organization of outstanding engineers. It is autonomous in its administration and in the selection of its members, sharing with the National Academy of Sciences the responsibility for advising the federal government. The National Academy of Engineering also sponsors engineering programs aimed at meeting national needs, encourages education and research, and recognizes the superior achievements of engineers. Dr. William A. Wulf is interim president of the National Academy of Engineering.

The Institute of Medicine was established in 1970 by the National Academy of Sciences to secure the services of eminent members of appropriate professions in the examination of policy matters pertaining to the health of the public. The Institute acts under the responsibility given to the National Academy of Sciences by its congressional charter to be an adviser to the federal government and, upon its own initiative, to identify issues of medical care, research, and education. Dr. Kenneth I. Shine is president of the Institute of Medicine.

The National Research Council was organized by the National Academy of Sciences in 1916 to associate the broad community of science and technology with the Academy's purposes of furthering knowledge and advising the federal government. Functioning in accordance with general policies determined by the Academy, the Council has become the principal operating agency of both the National Academy of Sciences and the National Academy of Engineering in providing services to the government, the public, and the scientific and engineering communities. The Council is administered jointly by both Academies and the Institute of Medicine. Dr. Bruce M. Alberts and Dr. William A. Wulf are chairman and interim vice chairman, respectively, of the National Research Council.

Support for this project was provided by the Administration for Children and Families of the U.S. Department of Health and Human Services.

ISBN 0-309-5649-7

Additional copies of this report are available from National Academy Press, 2101 Constitution Avenue, N.W., Lock Box 285, Washington, DC 20055
Call 1-800-624-6242 or 202-334-3313 (in the Washington metropolitan area).

This report is also available on-line at **http://www.nap.edu**

COMMITTEE ON YOUTH DEVELOPMENT

JOMILLS BRADDOCK *(Chair),* Department of Sociology, University of
  Miami
DAVID V.B. BRITT, Children's Television Workshop, New York
LINDA MARIE BURTON, Department of Human Development and Family
  Studies, Pennsylvania State University
DELBERT S. ELLIOTT, Center for the Study and Prevention of Violence,
  University of Colorado at Boulder
OTIS S. JOHNSON, Chatham-Savannah Youth Futures Authority, Savannah,
  Georgia
IRIS LITT, Division of Adolescent Medicine, Stanford University Medical
  Center
MILBREY MCLAUGHLIN, School of Education, Stanford University
TIMOTHY SANDOS, Government Affairs, TCI Central, Inc., Denver,
  Colorado
RALPH SMITH, Annie E. Casey Foundation, Baltimore, Maryland

ROSEMARY CHALK, *Staff Director*
KAREN AUTREY, *Project Assistant*

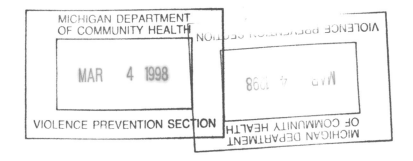

iv

Contents

Preface

Today's youth live and develop in a society that offers tremendous choices and challenges during the formative period of adolescence. The adolescent's environment is shaped profoundly by the presence or absence of many different factors, including family resources, community services, and educational and employment opportunities. In the past few decades, a body of social and behavioral research has emerged that seeks to explain why some adolescents successfully navigate their social settings, while others who are similarly situated adopt "risky" lifestyles characterized by drug use, unprotected sexual behavior, dropping out of school, delinquency, gang membership, and violence. During the same period, community leaders have experimented with a wide variety of approaches designed to improve the quality of life for all community residents, including the creation of social settings that are supportive of youth—schools, recreation centers, job training programs, and others.

The Administration for Children and Families (ACF) of the U.S. Department of Health and Human Services has contributed to these efforts by sponsoring community-based programs to enhance social and economic opportunities for adolescents as they develop to adulthood. At the request of ACF, the Committee on Youth Development of the Board on Children, Youth, and Families (which operates under the joint auspices of the National Research Council and the Institute of Medicine) convened a one-day workshop in January 1996. Chaired by Jomills Braddock, professor of sociology at the University of Miami, the committee developed the workshop to review the research literature on social settings and youth development, as well as selected experiences with community youth service programs. Meeting participants included research scientists, service providers, and representatives of public and private agencies that seek to improve outcomes for youth. The purpose of the workshop, titled "Youth Development and Neighborhood Influences," was to focus attention on what is known about environmental influences that interact with youth characteristics, family factors, and peer influences to foster or inhibit successful outcomes for adolescents. Consideration was also given to subsequent activities that would foster fledgling collaborations among those who develop, fund, and study initiatives aimed at improving youth outcomes.

Based on the workshop discussions, this report represents an exploratory effort to describe the processes by which communities and families interact during periods of adolescent development. This report also represents an important step in the evolution of the work of the Board on Children, Youth, and Families. It builds on the recommendations made in *Losing Generations* (National Research Council, 1993) and observations noted in *Violence in Urban America* (National Research Council, 1994). This project provides an important resource for the formation of the board's new Forum on Adolescence, which will continue to broaden the board's scope of work into the teenage years. In seeking to combine the worlds of science, policy, and practice, the board aims to extend the emerging portfolio of research and program efforts that are focused on adolescent behavior and, in particular, to improve existing relationships between those who study how adolescents interact with their communities and those who are engaged in efforts to improve youth outcomes.

Many individuals have contributed to this report of the Committee on Youth Development. The report benefitted enormously from the insightful comments provided by the workshop participants, who are listed at the end of this volume. The committee expresses its deep appreciation to them.

The contributions of Rosemary Chalk, staff director of the committee, and Karen Autrey, project assistant, are particularly appreciated. Other staff members who contributed to this report include Deborah Phillips, director of the Board on Children, Youth, and Families, and Anne Bridgman, program officer for communications. We also acknowledge the contributions of Janet Overton, whose editing improved the report.

This report was funded by the Administration for Children and Families of the U.S. Department of Health and Human Services. We are grateful to Ann Rosewater, Howard Rolston, and Hossein Faris within ACF for their support and thoughtful contribution to this effort. We appreciate ACF engaging the board to help chart new approaches in the field of youth development that will encourage bold thinking about the directions this relatively young field should take.

Sheldon H. White, Chair
Board on Children, Youth, and Families

Youth Development and Neighborhood Influences

Challenges and Opportunities

Summary

On January 25, 1996, the Committee on Youth Development of the Board on Children, Youth, and Families convened a workshop to examine the implications of research on social settings for the design and evaluation of programs that serve youth. The January workshop provided an opportunity for the committee to examine the strengths and limitations of existing research on interactions between social settings and adolescent development. This research has drawn attention to the importance of understanding how, when, and where adolescents interact with their families, peers, and unrelated adults in settings such as home, school, places of work, and recreational sites. This workshop builds on previous work of the National Research Council and reiterates its support for integrating studies of social settings into more traditional research on individual characteristics, family functioning, and peer relationships in seeking to describe and explain adolescent behavior and youth outcomes.

Not only does this report examine the strengths and limitations of research on social settings and adolescence and identify important research questions that deserve further study in developing this field, but it also explores alternative methods by which the findings of research on social settings could be better integrated into the development of youth programs and services. Specific themes include the impact of social settings on differences in developmental pathways, role expectations, and youth identity and decision-making skills, as well as factors that contribute to variations in community context.

Although the workshop participants agreed on the importance of social settings as key factors that affect youth development, they conceded that research is just beginning to consider the difficult problems of defining, measuring, and assessing such influences. There is a need to combine qualitative and quantitative research, foster the creation of multiple data sources, encourage the development of theoretical research and longitudinal studies, identify different patterns of behavior associated with ethnic and cultural practices, and develop forums to sustain collaboration among researchers, practitioners, and program sponsors.

This report describes an emerging focus in research on youth development, identifies key topics that deserve further analysis in shaping a research agenda for this field, and emphasizes the need for continued dialogue to draw on the expertise of research scientists and community leaders in designing new programs to enhance outcomes for youth.

Introduction

Concerns about the increasing involvement of many adolescents in high-risk behaviors have prompted a search for strategies and approaches that can guide youth away from unhealthy and unsafe practices and engage them in becoming productive members of society. This search has revealed many uncertainties in understanding how teenagers negotiate critical transitions, such as from school to work and from child to parent, the formation of self-identity, and the selection of life options. In situations in which communities must struggle with the problems of poverty, crime, drugs, and other negative influences, some youth are able to connect with social and economic networks that can help them become successful and productive adults. Others never gain access to or turn away from such networks.

In seeking to explain these variations in adolescent development, researchers have focused traditionally on personal characteristics, family relationships, and peer friendships. Such lines of inquiry suggest that these factors interact across multiple dimensions to influence youth outcomes. More recently, research scholars have noted that social settings represent a whole new area that has largely been ignored in traditional scholarship. The recent emphasis on social settings in youth development research has stimulated new lines of research inquiry and research methods designed to explore how individual, family, and peer relationships and outcomes are influenced by factors such as physical environment, economic opportunity structures, and ethnic and social networks, especially in urban areas characterized by concentrated poverty. Scholars are investigating relationships between types and density of social interactions, youth perceptions of positive and negative influences within their social and physical environments, and ways in which these relationships and perceptions are associated with the emergence of problem behaviors within communities (such as crime, gangs, substance abuse, child maltreatment, and teenage pregnancy). Although this field of study is relatively young and lacks well-established theories and comprehensive data sets, research on social setting factors and adolescent development has significant implications for the design and evaluation of programs that serve youth.

An emphasis on social settings compels service providers to move beyond a perspective that focuses on the deficits of today's youth (such as delinquency, drug use, teenage pregnancy, and violence) and to examine the density and quality of social interactions as well as demographic features and economic measures in assessing a community's resources. The emphasis on social context has stimulated a new agenda for program development and evaluation, one that stresses the importance of knowing how, when, and where adolescents interact with their families, peers, and unrelated adults in settings such as home, employment, recreation, and education.

Research on social settings has spurred interest in describing and explaining how the diverse strategies used by youth, families, neighborhoods, and ethnic groups reflect their efforts to deal with conditions of instability, adversity, limited resources, and social change. The emerging research has also called attention to the importance of understanding how youth themselves perceive assets and deficits within their social settings, including their perceptions of schooling, appropriate peers, and reference groups. Finally, the research on social settings has highlighted the need to integrate the youth development research literature with other research on community development and community organization (in the fields of economics, urban studies, anthropology, and sociology, for example) so that knowledge can inform efforts to build communities that are supportive and protective of their youth and families.

For these reasons, the Board on Children, Youth, and Families was asked by the Administration for Children and Families to convene a Committee on Youth Development to determine the need for an ongoing review of the research base that could contribute to a broad range of governmental and private foundation youth initiatives. The committee was asked specifically to examine research that could inform the development of comprehensive, community-wide initiatives intended to improve the life trajectories of at-risk youth in economically poor areas.

The Charge to the Committee

The Committee on Youth Development convened a workshop on January 25, 1996, to examine the research in the fields of youth development and neighborhood influences. Thirty individuals from academic research centers, government agencies, and private foundations concerned with youth development programs participated in the workshop. They met in Washington, D.C., to review recent research findings, highlight promising venues for further exchange of knowledge about and experience with social setting interactions involving adolescents, and examine the implications of this knowledge and expertise for use in the design and evaluation of a broad range of public and private youth initiatives.

Three key questions provided a framework for organizing the workshop:

(1) What new conceptual models are shaping studies of the community factors that influence the trajectories of youth development?

(2) What issues need to be resolved to design more accurate measures of the strengths and limitations of community resources and better assessments of their impact on youth outcomes?

(3) What mechanisms could better enable researchers and service providers to exchange knowledge and expertise about social setting factors that influence programs that serve youth?

The participants examined what is known about the types of supports that produce positive outcomes for youth, critical components and services within neighborhoods that make a difference in youth outcomes, and strategies by which research knowledge and practitioner experience can be integrated to improve the design and evaluation of community initiatives serving youth. The participants paid particular attention to comprehensive strategies of neighborhood change and community development that could improve outcomes for youth, particularly in disadvantaged areas. Such strategies include the creation of empowerment zones, community schools, gang prevention efforts, and programs that serve runaway or delinquent youth—see, for example, the gang prevention program announced by the Administration for Children and Families (U.S. Department of Health and Human Services, 1994).

In developing this summary report, the committee drew on the workshop and a small group of research studies that were included as background readings for the workshop participants. A comprehensive review of the literature on social settings and youth development was not included within the scope of this project. Many areas of relevant research—such as research on the biological processes of adolescent development, studies that offer in-depth and comparative descriptions of different minority cultures, and studies of processes of community organization and development—were not included in the one-day workshop. Statements in this report regarding the quality or findings of the research literature on social settings are derived from the workshop and committee discussions rather than from a thorough synthesis of the appropriate research literature.

Shifting Perspectives:
The Problem with Problem Orientations

During the workshop, participants observed that, in the past few decades, researchers have started to examine why some adolescents in low-income communities successfully navigate environmental challenges, while others, similarly situated, adopt lifestyles characterized by drug use, unprotected sexual behavior, dropping out of school, delinquency, gang membership, and violence. In a similar manner, researchers have sought to identify risk factors that foster problems for youth, as well as patterns of resiliency that protect them from risky lifestyles. This research has emphasized the need to examine the "whole" youth (a concept that describes the assets as well as the deficits of individual adolescents), rather than isolating selected problem behaviors associated with youth in difficult circumstances.

The emphasis on the whole youth has led to a new appreciation of the importance of physical and social settings on adolescent development and the ways in which positive as well as negative influences within these settings foster or inhibit constructive adult-youth interactions. Such research has stimulated interest in recognizing how adolescents themselves perceive role models of successful adult behavior, how they protect themselves during periods of danger or uncertainty, and how they seek out individuals or groups that constitute community assets capable of helping them become productive members of society. The settings approach has also stimulated interest in the influence that ethnicity or group networks can exercise in facilitating or discouraging the ways in which youth connect with the world of adults.

The workshop participants observed that many researchers engaged in these studies have grown dissatisfied with the constraints imposed by the problem orientation in research on adolescent behavior. The problem orientation imposes a deficit model that often masks the personal, family, or community strengths that constitute social assets to help youth navigate through troubled times. It leads to fragmentation in studying youth, placing greater emphasis on negative behaviors to the detriment of positive developments, and it can discourage collaborative efforts to identify common origins for problems that may co-occur among youth. Researchers have noted that the problem orientation has discouraged a search for measures that can assess positive developments in youth outcomes, in contrast to the negative measures that are often cited in media reports and studies of adolescent behavior.

The limitations of the problem-oriented perspective are also reflected in the fragmentation of numerous federal programs that address the needs of delinquent and at-risk youth. The President's Crime Prevention Council, for example, identified 50 separate federal programs that help communities help their youth, including major programs such as the Job Corps, the Summer Youth Employment and Training Program, community policing, programs for educationally disadvantaged children, and the Public Housing Urban Revitalization Program (President's Crime Prevention Council, 1995). The General Accounting Office (GAO) has identified 131 programs administered by 16 different departments and other agencies that seek to benefit at-risk or delinquent youth, the costs of which exceeded $4 billion in fiscal year 1995 (U.S. General Accounting Office, 1996). The creation of numerous federal programs to address the needs of youth within disadvantaged communities has raised questions about program efficiency, overlap, and duplication of effort (U.S. General Accounting Office, 1996). The GAO report concluded that Congress may want to reexamine the structure of these programs because many of them target the same clients, share the same goal, and provide similar services.

The efforts of some private foundations represent alternatives to problem-oriented approaches in responding to the needs of youth in disadvantaged communities. Many of these programs are designed to improve the social settings of at-risk youth through comprehensive neighborhood initiatives, such as the Annie E. Casey Foundation's Community Change for Youth Development project, the Ford Foundation's Neighborhood and Family Initiative and Quantum Opportunities Program, and the Foundation for Child Development's Neighborhood Research Grants Program. Although evaluations of the impact of these programs are limited, they represent an important body of experience in testing new models of community partnership and youth participation.

The Influence of Social Settings on Youth Development

The study panel that produced the 1993 National Research Council (NRC) report *Losing Generations* concluded that communities and institutions that surround adolescents, which include families, neighborhoods, schools, health systems, and employment and training centers, are increasingly challenged by changing social and economic conditions within the larger society (National Research Council, 1993). These conditions include the decline in economic security for poor and middle-class families, the increase in the number of single-parent households, and the rise in the number of neighborhoods with concentrated poverty that are spatially and socially isolated from middle- and working-class areas. Such trends place enormous stresses on public and private institutions and resources at a time when large numbers of children are entering adolescence. Over the past two decades, as the major settings of adolescent life have become increasingly beleaguered, the NRC panel observed that "increasing numbers of youths are falling into the juvenile justice system, the child welfare system, and other even more problematic settings" (National Research Council, 1993:2).

But understanding and demonstrating the impact of social settings on youth development are difficult tasks that require theory-building and instrumentation. Jencks and Mayer (1990) noted that a long-term commitment would be required from both the research and program-funding communities to understand the role and processes by which social settings influence adolescent behavior. Although theoretical work has begun to classify the potential mechanisms by which neighborhoods may influence the development of youth, empirical results that can document the impact of community influences remain limited.

In the report *Losing Generations*, the panel observed that efforts to improve

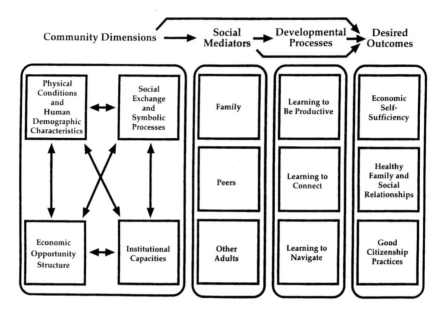

FIGURE 1   Components of conceptual framework.
SOURCE: Connell et al. (1995). Reprinted by permission.

the social settings of adolescents should strive to enable parents and community residents to increase their abilities to nurture young people. "Whether programs are offered in a single site or through interagency collaborations, their goal is to provide services that ensure that the emotional, recreational, academic, mental and physical health, and vocational needs of adolescents are explicitly addressed" (National Research Council, 1993:11). This conclusion was reinforced in the January 1996 workshop, which emphasized the need to improve connections between research and practice during periods of emerging research and programmatic experimentation.

Traditional disciplinary studies in sociology, anthropology, psychology, economics, and education, among other fields, are converging in the development of new theories that examine the characteristics of communities (opportunity structure, resources, social capital, change, and stability) that foster positive and negative developments for adolescents. Recognizing the dynamic, interactive, and multicontextual nature of youth experiences, workshop participants commented that the new conceptual frameworks emphasize the need for multiple lines of inquiry in this field and multiple levels of analysis (see Figure 1 for one example of a multilevel interactive framework presented in the workshop). They also identified several themes associated with this area of scholarship.

DIFFERENCES IN DEVELOPMENTAL PATHWAYS

One research study on youth has identified three key developmental tasks that characterize the period between early and late adolescence, ages 12 to 19 (Connell et al., 1995): learning to be productive, learning to connect, and learning to navigate. The participants indicated that, although these three tasks may be central to successful adolescent development, variations in experience and circumstances can influence their timing, sequencing, and relative importance at any given time. Participants observed that prevailing views of adolescent development and conceptual frameworks derived from white, middle-class adolescent populations may not reflect the experiences or unique challenges that confront youth who are influenced by other cultural traditions or by disadvantaged conditions.

Recent ethnographic research has alerted social scientists to the possibility that traditional theories of normative development do not necessarily provide the appropriate conceptual frameworks for studying the lives of inner-city teens. In a study of African American adolescents, for example, Burton et al. (1996) concluded that the developmental paths of those who grow up in poor, high-risk neighborhoods are based on ideologies, role expectations, behavioral practices, and rites of passage that provide a social context that differs from that commonly reported in studies of white suburban middle-class teens.

Several workshop participants mentioned other ethnographic research that suggests that inner-city, economically disadvantaged African American teenagers often experience an accelerated life course and are expected to become primary caretakers of siblings and younger relatives, adopt certain entrepreneurial skills to survive in their environments, and, in general, move quickly from childhood to adulthood. Many adolescents, in these environments, may neither experience nor perceive themselves to be within the transitional stage of adolescence. According to this line of research, adolescents who are compelled by economic or social circumstances to take on adult responsibilities in the area of family support, parenting, and child supervision may mature in ways that are quite different from other youth, but the developmental consequences of an accelerated life course are not yet known. The influence of ethnicity or race has been described primarily as a significant factor within the social context of African American teenagers, but it is also emerging in studies of other ethnic adolescents, including Hispanics and Asian American families.

THE IMPACT OF SETTINGS ON ROLE EXPECTATIONS

The strength and quality of social networks in economically advantaged or disadvantaged neighborhoods may affect the types of adult interactions that youth experience, which can influence their choice of role models and life course options. In some settings, schools, clubs, churches, sports teams, and other community groups recognize adolescence as a distinct, formative stage, and adults within these settings seek to prepare teenagers for adulthood. They consistently remind adolescents that although they are no longer children, they are not quite adults. Recognizing the importance of social supports for the accomplishment of key developmental tasks, several youth programs have sought to establish and enhance connective and supportive relationships between teenagers and adult mentors within disadvantaged communities. Workshop participants noted that evaluations of these programs have shown mixed results in areas such as academic performance, peer and family relationships, and illegal drug and alcohol use. As a result, uncertainty remains as to whether a developmental approach that stresses the importance of adult support and guidance during critical transition periods has the power to influence youth perceptions of life goals, decision-making skills, and outcomes.

Social settings that consistently provide negative messages about adolescent abilities and a limited range of desirable life options are thought to lead youth to make poor choices regarding the use of their time and resources. Several youth service programs are designed to move youth away from oppositional or alienated lifestyles and into support systems that can train and educate them to successfully be a part of mainstream society. But the research community needs to improve its ability to measure and assess the contributions of mentorship and other youth-development strategies, especially in circumstances in which mentorship programs must counter negative messages from other authority figures in the youth's social environment.

Family management practices and strategies to cope with risk may also be influenced by contextual variations regarding the extent and pervasiveness of crime or violence within communities. Caregivers may emphasize the importance of physical protection and security for children in dangerous neighborhoods (including restriction of the child's movements, strict curfews, and limited travel) and may choose to minimize strategies that foster individual autonomy and self-development for adolescents. The consequences of caregiving strategies associated with social settings can be profound: strategies that foster autonomy often encourage youth to move away from familiar environments and into new but unfamiliar social settings that can offer significant opportunities for growth.

Patterns of residential transience, often generated by poverty, represent another example of neighborhood factors that can influence youth development. Frequent household moves, disruptions in daily routines caused by unrelated individuals entering or departing the household, and mobility among neighbors can undermine community ties, weaken support networks, and reduce privacy. However, such transience does not inevitably disrupt development if adolescents have opportunities to sustain relationships with trusted adults.

SOCIAL MEDIATORS

Research on social settings has called attention to the role of unrelated adults who come into contact with youth in neighborhood and other social settings. Such individuals include teachers, mentors, coaches, employers, religious leaders, service providers, shop owners, and community leaders who may influence youth perceptions and behavior in their everyday settings. Researchers are exploring how the absence or presence of these individuals affect youth's perceptions of their own potential contributions and life options. Scholarship in this field has included both quantitative and qualitative studies; ethnographic studies in particular have described ways in which youth in inner-city communities interact with unrelated adults.

Workshop participants observed that a missing factor in the lives of youth in disadvantaged communities, especially in poor African American neighborhoods, is exposure to successful, upwardly mobile, mid-life adults (in the 30- to 50-year-old age range). Adults who become successful often move out of disadvantaged areas to higher-scale urban or suburban communities. Lacking this exposure, youth in at-risk neighborhoods may have limited opportunities to learn about strategies that involve family financial planning, balancing work and child care responsibilities, and the identification of educational and career opportunities across the life span. Workshop participants indicated that the movement of many middle- and upper-class individuals out of poor communities, along with the loss of many minority males because of early death or incarceration, has diminished the network of human resources within the community and reduced the opportunity for youth to interact with adults who can offer advice, support, perspective, and experience in negotiating school-to-work transitions, the initiation of sexual relations, and other key challenges during adolescence. Furthermore, the absence of employment settings, middle-class services (such as banks and supermarkets), and social investments in areas of concentrated poverty, combined with the presence of illicit markets and exposure to the social organization of illegitimate activities, can exacerbate the isolation of youth from socializing influences designed to generate adherence to positive social norms.

COMMUNITY CONTEXT

Neighborhood characteristics are increasingly viewed as part of the broader range of influences that can affect adolescents, although the magnitude of their impact is uncertain and difficult to measure. Characteristics that may influence youth development include (Carnegie Council on Adolescent Development, 1995, 1992; Connell et al., 1995; National Research Council, 1993; and Wilson, 1991):

- the decline in economic security (including decreasing real earnings and rising levels of unemployment), especially for young adults;

- the increase in single-parent, usually female-headed, families;
- the relation of male joblessness to social disorganization and rational planning for families and youth;
- easy access to illegal drugs and guns;
- rising rates of youth crime and juvenile detention; and
- the role of illegal or underground economies in providing for basic goods and services.

These contextual factors contribute to the absence of adult supervision and monitoring, a dearth of safe places to gather, the absence of constructive activities during idle periods, increased exposure to law enforcement and prison settings, and diminished opportunities for interaction between disadvantaged youth and middle- or upper-class professionals who can provide positive role models and institutional resources.

Variations in the community perceptions of contextual factors can be significantly influenced by the misuse of power and the effects of corruption within agencies or individuals who are supposed to be trusted. These variations are factors that can foster alienation, contempt, and an oppositional culture among young people, especially those who have limited contact with mainstream organizations and groups or who experience such contacts generally in a punitive fashion. The participants observed that these dynamics can directly affect adolescents' views of their own identity and the opportunities available to them, leading to growing isolation. The relationship between the "new" members of the community and the "old" residents can be positively or negatively influenced by perceptions of how each group relates to the neighborhood. For example, although tax and other financial incentives may attract middle-income families to purchase residences in areas characterized by poverty and transience, the housing authority, the school board, and county, municipal, and state governments may all have conflicting goals with respect to neighborhood initiatives. Middle-class families who have roots in a disadvantaged community and who are returning to improve the property and renew their roots may be welcomed. Such families may be resented, however, if they are seen as gentrifying invaders who bear few loyalties to the community or its residents.

Social and economic policies that foster commitment to community empowerment and neighborhood diversity can facilitate neighborhood improvement, but participants observed that variation in community development policies (such as mixed-income housing) is almost never considered in examining the implications of changing social and economic contexts on youth development. What is not known at present are the conditions under which social setting factors override other influences in a youth's environment, such as individual characteristics, child-parent relationships, and family functioning. The interactions that cause people to select the neighborhoods in which they reside need to be studied in comparison with interactions that are generated by the neighborhood itself. The variation that exists within neighborhoods may also reflect larger political and economic forces resulting from municipal, state, and national policies that shape neighborhood cultures.

Because of this variation, participants observed that lessons learned in dealing with positive or negative influences within one neighborhood may not be transferable to all others. Police patrols within disadvantaged communities may be regarded as assets or threats, for example, depending on the level of trust and confidence in law enforcement systems within the community. School systems may be regarded as negative factors if buildings are deteriorating and the quality of instruction is poor, or they may be seen as vital parts of the community if they provide important links to necessary services (such as health care and community resources).

Assessing Change and Development Within Neighborhoods

The scientific community is just beginning to develop tools to describe and assess relevant factors that influence the quality of life within neighborhoods. Researchers often rely on demographic data, census data, and property values as measures of social context, but these data provide few insights into contextual variations or the emergence of social strategies to cope with adversity within disadvantaged neighborhoods, especially over short time periods. Ethnographic research suggests that census tracts are not neighborhoods in any sociological sense, yet often census data provide the only empirical measure of neighborhood units in studies that seek to study communities over time. Measures that can assess the direction and rate of economic or social change within communities are particularly important in determining interim outcomes of community development programs as well as of programs designed to enhance successful outcomes for youth.

Despite the intensity of interest in neighborhood influences, this field of study is in its infancy. Quantitative research has not yet demonstrated a convincing association or established the causal pathways between social setting characteristics and adolescent development. Researchers are exploring alternative pathways to determine what measures should be employed in assessing the quality of "connectedness" between adolescents and the social and economic networks imbedded in their social settings.

The workshop participants noted that several key issues require attention to improve the measurement of the levels and quality of social networks:

- establishment of relevant community boundaries to facilitate longitudinal studies,
- creation of reliable and valid measures of the availability of and access to community services,
- selection of adequate community samples to obtain valid measures of resident experiences,
- factoring in the importance of timing in assessing patterns of deterioration and growth in urban environments,
- examining the pathways by which ethnicity and racial heritage influence social settings, and
- assessing unclear processes that connect physical and social environments within communities.

In developing these measures, participants noted that research on social context needs to consider more than physical factors in neighborhood settings. The types and levels of social interactions within a community involve dynamic and interpersonal elements that may reflect components such as the quality of services and institutions, levels of trust and security, homogeneity and density of friendship networks, flow of information and resources, coherence of values and perceptions among community residents, and opportunities for power and influence. Researchers are now examining how to identify and capture the critical dimensions of these factors and to explain how they interact to make neighborhoods a "good" or "bad" place in which to raise children.

Researchers are also increasingly interested in identifying measures that can capture the social and economic diversity within neighborhoods. Educational and employment opportunities, in particular, are not randomly distributed and may depend on friendship networks, access to transportation, and issues of safety and security as well as more traditional variables such as the strength of the school faculty and curriculum and job skills. All poor neighborhoods are not the same, participants observed. Economically deprived communities with high levels of social organization can provide consistent messages to their youth regarding the importance of becoming a successful, productive adult. In contrast, communities that share demographic and economic characteristics but experience low levels of trust, security, and shared values can send ambiguous or mixed messages to youth that reduce their chances for academic success and productive employment.

The participants cautioned that levels of social organization are themselves influenced by macrostructural forces that shape communities, such as industrial restructuring, shifts in employment opportunities, patterns of racial segregation, and changes in inflation rates and health-care costs. These factors provide the backdrop against which communities, families, and adolescents seek to enhance their strengths and reduce their risks, especially during periods of transition and change.

THE SIGNIFICANCE OF BOUNDARIES IN
COMMUNITY MEASURES

One theoretical construct that the workshop participants addressed was the need for ways to define consistent boundaries in the neighborhoods and social environments of today's youth. Social science research in a variety of fields (including youth development, child care, violence prevention, family management, and use of human services) has indicated that existing units that define community boundaries for statistical purposes (census tract data, zip code, or block group), although commonly used in research on social settings, may not demonstrate the dimensions of neighborhoods that have meaning for their residents. These predetermined boundaries can differ from resident-perceived boundaries in many neighborhoods. In communities characterized by high rates of social disorganization and social problems, including youth crime, drug trafficking, child maltreatment, unemployment, and vacant and transient housing, residents are more likely to disagree about what boundaries constitute the "neighborhood."

Consistent and meaningful boundaries are crucial to the development of studies that rely on quantitative and qualitative measures of change or stability in order to demonstrate neighborhood-level influences on human development. For these reasons, researchers within the social sciences are exploring how to improve theories, methods, and research instruments that can provide insights about the identification of spatial boundaries that reflect shared values, common experiences, and the convergence of residential standards (both environmental and social).

THE EFFECTS OF MULTIPLE SOCIAL SETTINGS ON
YOUTH DEVELOPMENT

An additional methodological challenge in assessing the impact of social settings is the fact that adolescents move among multiple contexts that are often defined by roles, functions, and expectations that differ from those of adults. Youth today are highly mobile—they may reside in one neighborhood, attend school in another, socialize with peers in a third, and be employed in a fourth. The interactive effects of these different contextual settings have not been analyzed, although the workshop participants observed that the social interactions and normative standards that shape each environment may influence youth development.

One mediating factor that requires further analysis in this area is the degree of consistency in role expectations attached to adolescents across diverse contexts and cultures. The concept of "good fit," in which the individual characteristics of youth satisfy the expectations of their social context (Lerner and Lerner, 1983), is based on an assumption that the multiple environments of youth encourage similar expectations for positive development. When role expectations diverge, youth may experience a broader range of messages regarding expected behavior and face more difficulty in perceiving or adhering to normative directions. Ethnographers have noted that mixed messages and role conflicts are commonly associated with school/family environments in the lives of African American youth, particularly those who must bear adult burdens of child care or full-time jobs to support their families. Within the workshop discussion, participants observed that such conflicts can also surface in home/workplace environments, as youth realize that they must compete with older relatives for limited employment opportunities.

THE IMPORTANCE OF MULTIPLE DATA SOURCES

In assessing measures of community change, the participants observed that multiple data sources are necessary to provide insight into the heterogeneity and interactive dimensions of social settings. Survey and interview data, which are commonly used to obtain residents' observations about their communities, need to be accompanied by research materials that have external validity, either through observational reports or administrative data and records. Together, ethnographic and quantitative studies can provide a richer and more detailed research strategy than that which can be obtained by a single methodological approach.

The participants also urged that researchers give attention to the range of variation or consistency within community expectations, norms, aspirations, and sanctions (especially in areas such as child care roles, adult supervision, care of elderly or other dependent relatives, family support, and availability of economic opportunities) in judging the overall quality of a social environment.

SAMPLING AND TIMING IN MEASURES OF COMMUNITY CHANGE

The dynamic and interactive nature of social settings requires caution in developing appropriate measurement instruments, the participants noted. It is important to know whose perspective counts—especially among youth—in constructing valid residential samples.

For example, in assessing the impact of community development efforts, the design and timing of survey studies, interviews, and evaluations can be critical in determining whether a selected intervention has reached the appropriate stage of implementation. The participants noted that individual and group samples need to be constructed that illustrate the range of variation within and between communities, especially in assessing the impact of short- and long-term socioeconomic changes, the quality of services and strength of institutions, the forms and degree of involvement of community members, and the extent of social alienation of individuals, groups, and neighborhoods.

IMPLICATIONS FOR RESEARCH DESIGN

Many insights regarding the impact of social settings on youth development have been derived from ethnographic studies that describe the quality of life, the level of trust among neighbors, and other factors that foster or discourage the creation of cohesive social units. Qualitative research has been helpful in generating new hypotheses and conceptual models that can describe the processes of change that accompany neighborhood growth or deterioration. But the predictive capacities of these models are limited and few opportunities exist to study interactive social patterns within and between communities over time.

The workshop participants noted that a new generation of neighborhood studies is under way, based on integrated, multidisciplinary, life-span models of neighborhood effects. Yet research opportunities are needed to integrate longitudinal surveys and ethnographic data collection to provide multiple sources for data analysis and to enhance descriptions and comparisons of multidimensional, life-course trajectories for youth in disadvantaged environments.

As this research moves forward, greater effort will be needed to: (a) integrate quantitative and qualitative studies, (b) develop research instruments and theoretical models that can identify and measure specific aspects of social interactions within and between neighborhoods, and (c) support longitudinal studies that can analyze multiple social factors in community settings over time. Such instruments and models would allow the research community to gain insights into the health or deterioration of selected communities, examine the impact of specific social settings (such as schools, detention centers, sports teams, and so forth) on peer and adult relationships, and explore their influence on youth development.

The Need for Informed Conversations
Between Research and Practice

Recognizing areas of convergence in both conceptual theories and program experience, scholars and practitioners have begun to synthesize lessons learned from the emerging research base as well as from federal, state, and local programs that serve youth, in order to identify key factors that influence how youth move into pathways that encourage them to become productive, nurturing, and contributing adults. In considering the implications of research on social settings in program design and future research studies, the workshop participants stressed the need for new forms of informed conversations, collaboration, and partnerships between research scientists and service providers in the areas of community and youth development.

EXISTING PARTNERSHIPS AND COLLABORATIONS

In reviewing the need for new forums to foster dialogue and collaboration between the research and practice communities, the participants observed that several partnership efforts already are in place. Several "bridging organizations" have emerged, for example, to facilitate dialogues within and between programs focused on youth services and community development. Such efforts include the National Community-Building Network, schools of graduate education in the fields of social policy and human services that link research and practice, educational programs that offer in-depth training for service providers, and electronic networks such as HANDS.NET and the comprehensive strategies forum that offer on-line access to program experiences and perspectives.

Several research collaboration networks have also emerged to help integrate the findings from studies by individual researchers. Examples of such networks include the studies on poverty, neighborhoods, and child development organized within the Social Science Research Council and the MacArthur Foundation Network on Successful Adolescent Development.

INTEGRATION OF RESEARCH AND PRACTICE

Although some efforts to create multiagency and multidisciplinary approaches addressing the relationships between youth development and neighborhood influences are under way, participants observed that these approaches offer few opportunities to examine basic conceptual models that accompany program design and implementation. A critical, ongoing examination of emerging theories, instrumentation, and research findings could help integrate efforts to strengthen social organization within disadvantaged communities, improve programs designed to enhance positive outcomes for youth, and create ongoing dialogues between individual program efforts and research studies.

In addition, better links need to be established between service providers and researchers within community and youth development efforts that engage three types of programs: (a) community-building programs, designed to attract investment capital, regulate land-use patterns, and enhance economic opportunities; (b) social service programs, designed to enhance the quality of community services in areas such as health, safety, and education; strengthen informal social networks; and improve the quality of life within depressed regions; and (c) youth-oriented programs, designed to enhance positive outcomes for youth by addressing their basic developmental needs.

The emerging research on the influence of social settings on youth outcomes, as well as new conceptual models and measures focused on processes of variation and change within communities, has stimulated interest in creating additional opportunities for the exchange of knowledge and expertise. The workshop participants noted that this exchange requires not only interdisciplinary approaches that can draw on different areas of research scholarship, but also the creation of forums that can foster sustained interchanges among researchers, service providers, and other community leaders (such as those affiliated with business, religious, and political organizations) who have extensive experience in working with youth or neighborhoods and who understand the types of interactions that characterize the social settings of today's adolescents.

The workshop participants observed that this exchange of knowledge and perspectives is important for several reasons:

• Emerging research on social context factors and interactions offers an important opportunity to examine the variations within settings that can directly contribute to youth outcomes;

- This research base can contribute to the design and assessment of community-based programs intended to improve youth outcomes;
- The relatively recent origins of research on social settings suggest that significant modifications and improvements in the conceptual frameworks and research measures should be expected in the coming decade;
- The practitioner community has experience and perspectives that are critical to the development of useful theory and measures regarding the role and impact of social settings and social interactions;
- The multidisciplinary character of the emerging research scholarship will require intensive training programs and bridging efforts focused on understanding and improving outcomes for youth; and
- The patchwork of programs that has been assembled over the past few decades to assist children, youth, and families is now in flux as policy officials and service providers in a variety of organizational settings seek to provide human services and supports in a more comprehensive, coordinated manner.

Workshop participants observed that the time is ripe to describe the experiences and insights associated with efforts to change the quality and nature of educational, health, and social service systems; to examine the variation within different community experiments; and to develop data collection efforts that can assess their impact on youth outcomes over time.

Next Steps

In outlining steps that could be taken to foster the exchange of expertise among representatives of research, policy, and practice at the national and local levels, the workshop participants offered several observations to guide the development of future efforts in this field. They noted that several steps are needed to enhance the integration of emerging research on social settings in the design of programmatic efforts:

1. Advances in research need to be directed toward demonstrating the pathways and conditions under which social settings affect youth development, as well as the ways in which social settings are perceived and influenced by the youth who reside within them. Theory-building and methodological innovations are needed to develop more powerful approaches to capture the complexity of social interactions and specific mechanisms that can explain different developmental sequences and trajectories over time, as well as the variation in youth outcomes within communities that share common features. Although some promising methods do exist (such as hierarchial linear modeling and growth curve and life event analysis), they have limited capacity for describing multidimensional life course trajectories or developmental outcomes in multiple contextual settings. In this area, attention must be given to strengthening research in ethnic minority communities, in order to capture the norms and adaptation processes characteristic of different cultures and to discern important factors and processes that facilitate or discourage youth in becoming successful adults.

Efforts to integrate ethnographic and quantitative studies will need to address the long history of misunderstandings among investigators who employ these two approaches. A central challenge is that of articulating how carefully sequenced, multimethod research can reveal the interplay between developmental processes and social interactions within communities. Comparative ethnographies (studies of neighborhoods conducted simultaneously across multiple sites), as well as research that uses both quantitative and ethnographic methods, offer critical contributions to theory-building, the design of research instruments and data collection, and ultimately the design and refinement of approaches to foster constructive youth development.

2. The embryonic work on social settings warrants systematic efforts to orchestrate joint knowledge-building efforts among those who design, study, and evaluate youth service and community development programs. Although still incomplete, research on the diversity and quality of youth relationships with peers and adults in different social settings has the potential to offer important insights for program strategies and outcome assessments in youth service agencies. Research on the time spent in different social settings can illustrate the diversity of experiences that youth confront in their daily lives. Identifying components and strategies within successful communities that support positive outcomes for youth is a common goal within both the research and service provider enterprise.

The increasing specialization of the research community has created a need for strategies designed to broaden the dialogue among disciplines, experiment with new forms of research design and data collection, and foster reward systems and a culture that encourage collaborative efforts between research and practice.

3. Experience with youth development research and programs, including research on social settings, should be integrated with other community development efforts. Investments in social strategies and community resources that can promote youth development will require more attention to the types of social resources that youth seek out and create, as well as consideration of the ways in which youth gain information and control over their environment. These efforts need to be integrated with other community development initiatives, such as special economic investment initiatives and health and social services (including housing, education, and recreational facilities) designed to enhance the capacity of communities to achieve the goals of their residents. The creation of special programs or demonstration projects can help foster the development of healthy neighborhoods, but such enhancement efforts need to become part of the natural set of daily relationships within the neighborhood so they can be sustained over time. The successful blending of different social classes within "poor" or "dangerous" communities to achieve diversity and heterogeneity among youth and adults within informal social organizations and personal relationships is a particular challenge that requires attention.

Many generations created the neighborhood environments that surround today's youth, and quick fixes cannot be expected for problems that were more than a half century in the making. As public and private agencies prepare their strategies and program plans for the decade ahead and consider alternative methods of investment in jobs, schools, child care, health care, and housing, the field of youth development will continue to gain attention. The growing social antagonism toward youth, driven by perceptions of a youth crime wave and youthful predators, suggests that punitive as well as supportive measures will gain increased support. Demographic trends indicate that a large cohort of youth will move through adolescence during a time when society is experiencing major changes in its social and economic policies, highlighting the need for strategies that can offer positive guidance during times of conflicting messages and uncertain futures. The time is ripe for informed action to add to an emerging knowledge base and to enhance program opportunities for building communities that can support their youth.

References

Burton, L.M., D.O. Obeidallah, and K. Allison
  1996 Ethnographic insights on social context and adolescent development among inner-city African-American teens. In R. Jessor, A. Colby, and R. Shweder (eds.), *Essays on Ethnography and Human Development.* Chicago: University of Chicago Press.
Carnegie Council on Adolescent Development
  1995 *Great Transitions: Preparing Adolescents for a New Century.* October. New York: Carnegie Corporation of New York.
  1992 *A Matter of Time: Risk and Opportunity in the Nonschool Hours.* Task Force on Youth Development and Community Programs. New York: Carnegie Corporation of New York.
Connell, J.P., J.L. Aber, and G. Walker
  1995 How do urban communities affect youth? Social science research to inform the design and evaluation of comprehensive community initiatives. In J.P. Connell et al. (eds.), *New Approaches to Evaluating Community Initiatives.* Washington, DC: The Aspen Institute.
Jencks, C., and S. Mayer
  1990 The social consequences of growing up in a poor neighborhood. In L.E. Lynn and M.G.H. McGeary (eds.), *Inner-city Poverty in the United States.* Committee on National Urban Policy, National Research Council. Washington, DC: National Academy Press.
Lerner, J.V., and R.M. Lerner
  1983 Temperament and adaptation across life: Theoretical and empirical issues. In P.B. Baltes and O.G. Brin, Jr. (eds.), *Life-Span Development and Behavior.* Vol. 5. New York: Academic Press.
National Research Council
  1993 *Losing Generations: Adolescents in High-Risk Settings.* Panel on High-Risk Youth, National Research Council. Washington, DC: National Academy Press.
  1994 *Violence in Urban America: Mobilizing a Response.* Committee on Law and Justice, National Research Council. Washington, DC: National Academy Press.

President's Crime Prevention Council
1995 *Preventing Crime and Promoting Responsibility: 50 Programs that Help Communities Help Their Youth.* September. Washington, DC: U.S. Government Printing Office.

U.S. Department of Health and Human Services
1994 Youth Gang Drug Prevention Program. Administration for Children and Families. Program Announcement No. ACF-94-X. *Federal Register* 59(88):23867-23877.

U.S. General Accounting Office
1996 At-Risk and Delinquent Youth. GAO/HEHS-96-34. March.

Wilson, W.J.
1991 Studying inner city dislocations: The challenges of public agenda research. *American Sociological Review* 45:1-14.

APPENDIX

Workshop Participants

J. LAWRENCE ABER, National Center for Children in Poverty, Columbia University

ELIJAH ANDERSON, Department of Sociology, University of Pennsylvania

JOMILLS BRADDOCK (*Chair*),* Department of Sociology, University of Miami

DAVID V.B. BRITT,* Children's Television Workshop, New York

LINDA BURTON,* Department of Human Development and Family Studies, Pennsylvania State University

ROSEMARY CHALK, Board on Children, Youth, and Families, National Research Council

JAMES CONNELL, Institute for Research and Reform in Education, Philadelphia

CLAUDIA COULTON, Center for Urban Poverty and Social Change, Case Western Reserve University

ANGELA DURAN, Office of the Assistant Secretary for Planning and Evaluation, U.S. Department of Health and Human Services

DELBERT ELLIOTT,* Center for the Study and Prevention of Violence, University of Colorado at Boulder

HOSSEIN FARIS, Office of Policy and Evaluation, Administration for Children and Families, U.S. Department of Health and Human Services

---

*Committee member

RON FERGUSON, John F. Kennedy School of Government, Harvard University
MARCIA FESTEN, John D. and Catherine T. MacArthur Foundation, Chicago
ANDREW HAHN, Heller Graduate School for Advance Studies in Social Policy, Brandeis University
KAREN HEIN, Institute of Medicine, National Academy of Sciences
HELEN HOWERTON, Division of Child and Family Development, Office of Planning, Research and Evaluation, Administration for Children and Families, U.S. Department of Health and Human Services
OTIS JOHNSON,* Chatham-Savannah Youth Futures Authority, Savannah, Georgia
ELISA KOFF, Office of the Assistant Secretary for Planning and Evaluation, U.S. Department of Health and Human Services
TERRY LEWIS, Family and Youth Services Bureau, Administration for Children, Youth and Families, U.S. Department of Health and Human Services
MILBREY MCLAUGHLIN,* School of Education, Stanford University
FAITH MITCHELL, Division on Social and Economic Studies, Commission on Behavioral and Social Sciences and Education, National Research Council
INCA MOHAMED, Ford Foundation, New York
EMILY NOVICK, Office of the Assistant Secretary for Planning and Evaluation, U.S. Department of Health and Human Services
DEBORAH A. PHILLIPS, Board on Children, Youth, and Families, National Research Council
HOWARD ROLSTON, Office of Policy and Evaluation, Administration for Children and Families, U.S. Department of Health and Human Services
ANN ROSEWATER, Office of the Deputy Assistant Secretary, Administration for Children and Families, U.S. Department of Health and Human Services
TIMOTHY SANDOS,* Government Affairs, TCI Central, Inc., Denver, Colorado
LONNIE SHERROD, William T. Grant Foundation, New York
RALPH SMITH,* Annie E. Casey Foundation, Baltimore, Maryland
PAM STEVENS, DeWitt Wallace-Readers' Digest Fund, New York
BARBARA BOYLE TORREY, Commission on Behavioral and Social Sciences and Education, National Research Council